W9-AAD-064

Frogs
and Other Amphibians

Book Author: Sheri Reda
For World Book:
Editorial: Paul A. Kobasa, Scott Thomas, Christine Sullivan
Research: Cheryl Graham
Graphics and Design: Sandra Dyrlund, Brenda Tropinski
Photos: Tom Evans
Permissions: Janet Peterson
Indexing: David Pofelski
Proofreading: Tina Ramirez
Pre-press and Manufacturing: Carma Fazio, Anne Fritzinger, Steve Hueppchen

**For information about other World Book publications, visit our Web site at
http://www.worldbookonline.com or call 1-800-WORLDBK (967-5325). For information about sales
to schools and libraries, call 1-800-975-3250 (United States); 1-800-837-5365 (Canada).**

World Book, Inc.
233 N. Michigan Avenue
Chicago, IL 60601
U.S.A.

The Library of Congress has cataloged an earlier edition of this title as follows:

Frogs and other amphibians.
    p. cm. -- (World Book's animals of the world)
    Includes bibliographical references and index.
    ISBN 0-7166-1269-0   5444
    1. Frogs--Juvenile literature. 2. Amphibians--Juvenile literature.
I. World Book, Inc. II. Series.
QL668 .E2F774 2005
597.8--dc22
                                2004007543

This edition:
Frogs: ISBN-10: 0-7166-1297-6   ISBN-13: 978-0-7166-1297-1
Set 4: ISBN-10: 0-7166-1285-2   ISBN-13: 978-0-7166-1285-8

Printed in Malaysia
3 4 5 6 7 8 09 08 07

Picture Acknowledgments: Cover: Michael S. Bisceglie, Animals Animals; © Jane Burton, Bruce Coleman Collection; © National
Geographic Society/Getty Images; © Juan Manuel Renjifo, Animals Animals; © Linda Richardon, Corbis.

© Michael S. Bisceglie, Animal Animals 51; © Jane Burton, Bruce Coleman Collection 55; © Suzanne L. Collins & Joseph T.
Collins, Photo Researchers 43; © Stephen Dalton, Photo Researchers 5, 25; © Michael Durham 61; © Tom Edwards, Animals,
Animals 19; © Michael & Patricia Fogden, Corbis 11; © The Image Bank/Getty Images 3, 15; © Kitchin & Hurst, Tom Stack &
Associates 5, 7, 21; © Dwight R. Kuhn 45; © Carmela Leszczynski, Animals Animals 29; © S.R. Maglione, Photo Researchers
41; © Joe McDonald, Corbis 31; © Tom McHugh, Photo Researchers 37; 13; © Gary Meszaros, Photo Researchers 48; © Gary
Nafis 49; © National Geographic Society/Getty Images 23; © Ralph Reinhold, Animals Animals 33; © Juan Manuel Renjifo,
Animals Animals 59; Linda Richardson, Corbis 4, 39; © Austin J. Stevens, Animals Animals 13; Kim Taylor, Bruce Coleman Inc.
53; Doug Wechsler, Animals Animals 27, 35.

Illustrations: WORLD BOOK illustrations by John Fleck 10, 17, 22.

World Book's Animals of the World

Frogs
and Other Amphibians

Clifton Park - Halfmoon Public Library
475 Moe Road
Clifton Park, New York 12065

WORLD
BOOK

a Scott Fetzer company
Chicago
www.worldbookonline.com

Contents

I hope I can hold on to this tail! I lost the last two!

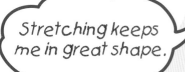

Stretching keeps me in great shape.

I'm no tasty morsel!

What Is an Amphibian?

An amphibian *(am FIB ee uhn)* is an animal that usually lives part of its life in water and part of its life on land. Frogs and toads, salamanders, and caecilians *(see SIHL ee uhns)* are amphibians.

Most amphibians begin life as larvae *(LAHR vee)*. The larvae hatch out of eggs that their mothers laid in water or in a very wet area. Then most of the larvae go through metamorphosis *(meht uh MOR fuh sis)*. That means their bodies and the way they live change. During metamorphosis, young amphibians grow into adults. Adult amphibians usually look very different from larvae.

Some amphibians continue to live in the water after they reach adulthood. But most adult amphibians spend their lives on land, although they usually return to the water when they want to mate and lay eggs.

6

Green frog

Where in the World Do Frogs and Other Amphibians Live?

Frogs have lived on Earth for about 180 million years, and they've developed ways to live on every continent of the world except Antarctica. Today, most frogs live in tropical regions.

Different kinds of frogs live in different habitats. Members of the common group of frogs, known as "true frogs," usually live in or near water. They have long hind legs, smooth skin, and webbed hind feet.

Tiny tree frogs dwell in—you guessed it—trees. Other frogs live on rocky cliffs, or in swift mountain streams. Some kinds of frogs live in burrows and eat ants and termites.

Many kinds of frogs and other amphibians live their whole lives in or near water. But some leave the water when they become adults and only return to mate and lay eggs or bear their young. A few types of frogs never enter the water.

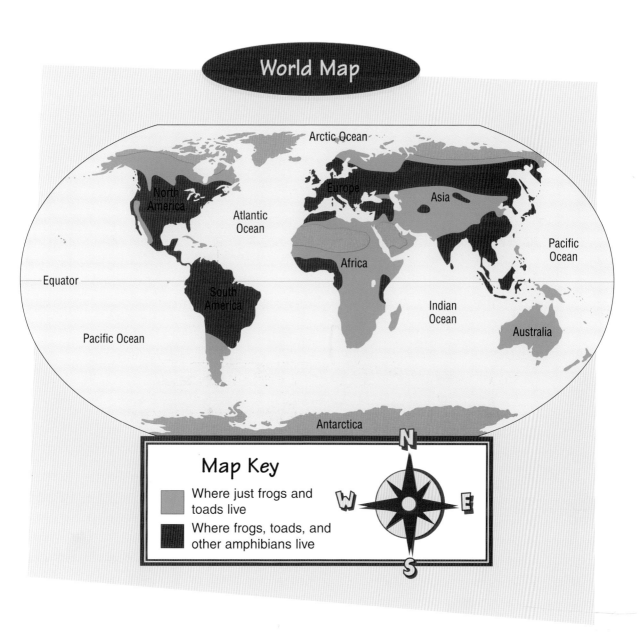

World Map

Arctic Ocean

North America

Atlantic Ocean

Europe

Asia

Africa

Pacific Ocean

Equator

South America

Indian Ocean

Pacific Ocean

Australia

Antarctica

Map Key

Where just frogs and toads live

Where frogs, toads, and other amphibians live

N
W E
S

9

Is That Thing a Frog?

A tadpole doesn't look much like a frog—but when it grows up, that's exactly what it will be. Most types of frogs spend the first stage of life as tadpoles, which is simply another name for frog larvae.

Tadpoles hatch out of eggs that are covered by a thick, jellylike coat that keeps them moist. At first, tadpoles look a lot like fish. They have gills, lidless eyes, and finlike tails for swimming.

Some kinds of tadpoles go through metamorphosis in about 10 days. Others take as long as two years to change form completely.

During metamorphosis, a tadpole first grows hind legs. Then forelegs appear from under the gills. The mouth widens and a tongue develops. Then the lungs develop and the gills disappear. The skin gets thicker and tougher, nostrils form, and the body absorbs the tail: it disappears! The tadpole has become a frog.

adult frog

tadpoles

eggs

Tadpoles

Why Are Frogs So Cold?

Like all amphibians, frogs are ectotherms (*EHK tuh thuhrmz*). They can't warm themselves up or cool themselves off. They have to rely on their habitat to do that for them.

People say frogs are cold-blooded animals, but their blood isn't really cold. Their body temperature tends to be the same as the temperature of the surrounding air or water.

When the weather gets too hot and dry, frogs often estivate *(EHS tih vayt)*, or sleep underground away from the heat. When they sense moisture in the soil, they awaken and come to the surface.

Frogs that live in areas that have winter hibernate *(HI buhr nayt)* to escape the cold. They may burrow under leaves or mud at the bottom of a pond or stream. Or they may dig down as much as a foot underground, often under rocks or rotten logs.

Bullfrog emerging from the mud

Are All Frogs Green?

Not all frogs are green. Frogs can be green, gray, red, blue, yellow, purple, orange, or combinations of two or more colors. Whether their skin is plain or eye-catching, it serves as an adaptation: it helps them stay safe.

Some frogs use their skin as camouflage, to help them blend into their environment. Certain frogs even change their skin color with changes in humidity, light, and temperature.

Highly toxic frogs display bright colors to warn predators *(PRED uh tuhrz)* not to eat them. And some nontoxic frogs display bright colors so predators will think they're poisonous, too.

Frogs shed the outer layer of their skin many times a year. So do toads. They use their forelegs to pull the old skin off over their heads. Then they eat it!

Tree frog and
horned frog

15

What's Under All That Thin, Wet Skin?

A frog is a vertebrate, or an animal with a backbone. Like other vertebrates, a frog also has organs, such as a heart, a liver, kidneys, and lungs.

But a frog is different from other vertebrates. A frog's heart has three chambers, not four. Frogs can breathe through their skin as well as their lungs.

All frogs have the same basic body structure. They have short front legs and flat heads and bodies. After they grow out of the tadpole stage, frogs don't have tails.

Most frogs have large back legs, which help them hop from place to place. But a few frogs that dig burrows have short hind legs. They can't hop at all.

Diagram of a Frog

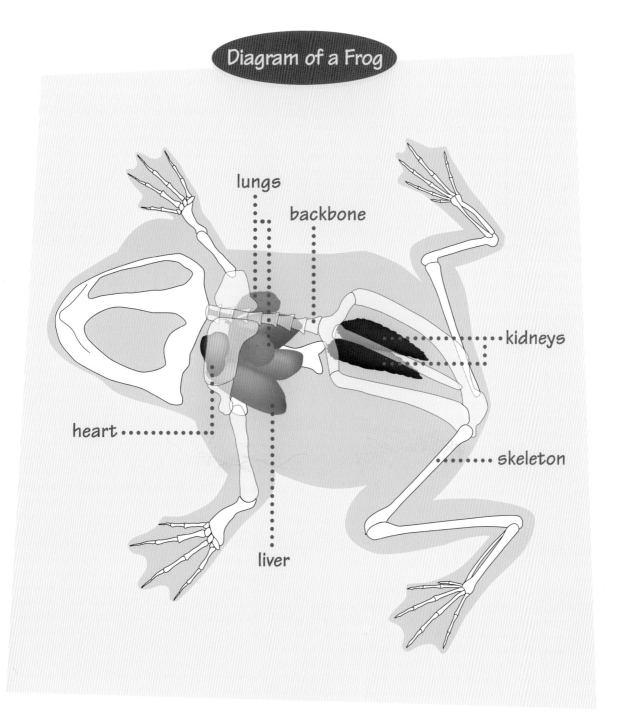

lungs

backbone

kidneys

heart

skeleton

liver

How Do Frogs Protect Themselves?

In addition to coloration that camouflages them or warns that they're poisonous, frogs have good eyesight. They also have a delicate sense of touch to help them keep track of their surroundings.

If a predator spots a frog, the frog might play dead because most predators prefer live food. If it's too late to hide or play dead, a frog may try to scare its enemy and get away. For example, some tree frogs flash brilliant colors to startle their enemies. Budgett's frog of Argentina and Paraguay bellows, screams, and grunts to scare foes away.

Frogs that live on the ground or in water have powerful legs that can help them hop or swim away from predators. Tree frogs can escape danger by leaping from branch to branch. Flying frogs don't actually fly, but they can jump right out of trees and glide to safer places.

Camouflaged gray tree frog hiding under bark

Are Some Frogs Poisonous?

Most frogs are harmless, but some frogs, as well as some toads, have glands that ooze poison onto their skin. The poison dart frogs of Central and South America make a poison on their skin strong enough to kill almost any predator. Indians in this region have painted this poison on arrows to make them deadly.

Most of the other kinds of poisonous frogs emit only a mild poison. Some of these frogs simply taste so bad because of the poison that no one wants to eat them. But others are deadly to small predators. Often, the brighter the frog is, the more deadly the poison it emits.

Mildly poisonous frogs are usually harmless to humans, but even mild poisons can irritate your eyes. Be sure to wash your hands after handling a frog. Also, keep frogs and toads away from pets. Poison that may only irritate a human could have a worse effect on a smaller animal.

Strawberry poison
dart frog

Are All Frog Feet the Same?

Different kinds of frogs have different kinds of feet. Frogs that live in or near water have webbed toes on their hind feet. The webbing helps them swim quickly through the water.

Flying frogs, which glide from tree to tree, have extra webbing on their front and hind feet. This extra webbing helps the frogs glide through the air.

Some tree frogs have no webbing at all on their feet. Instead, these frogs have sticky pads on the ends of their toes. The pads help them cling to the surface of tree trunks, twigs, and leaves as they climb.

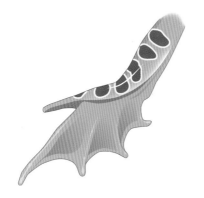
webbed toes

nonwebbed toes

Flying frog on a log

How Far Can Frogs Jump?

Some frogs can make impressive jumps. Many frogs can leap 20 times their own body length. Some tree frogs can jump over 7 feet (2 meters). That's nearly 50 times their body length. That is like a 6-foot (1.8-meter) human jumping 300 feet (90 meters)!

Not all frogs are great jumpers, however. Some frogs that dig burrows, for example, have short hind legs. Many of them hop weakly, if at all.

Tree frog leaping

How Do Frogs Find Mates?

During breeding season, when they want to find a mate, frogs often return to the place where they hatched. Usually, the males arrive first. Each male croaks loudly to establish its own territory.

In many species, when the females arrive, the males puff up vocal sacs in their throats and make a special mating call. They wait for females to respond.

After a female chooses a male, he climbs onto her back and holds onto her in the water. The female lays eggs and the male produces a milky substance that is poured over the eggs to fertilize *(FURH tuhl lyz)* them.

Tree frog singing

What Do Frogs Eat?

Frogs in the wild will eat almost anything they can catch—but only if it's still alive. Most frogs eat insects, snails, and tadpoles. Large frogs will also eat small mammals, birds, fish, and reptiles.

Most frogs have a keen ability to spot movement. Once a frog recognizes a moving object as prey, it tries to catch it. Some frogs can flick their tongues out in a fraction of a second to grab their food. Other frogs use their jaws to trap their prey.

In the water, a frog may simply open its mouth and gulp its prey. Like most other amphibians, frogs have teeth. But they only use them to grip food, not to chew it. If a frog catches something that tastes bad, it spits it out. But if the frog likes its catch, it swallows it whole.

Tree frog swallowing
a cricket

How Do Frogs Help Humans?

Frogs are helpful to humans in a number of ways. Frogs eat many insects that are pests, such as mosquitoes and flies. They also eat insects that harm crops.

In addition, because their bodies are so similar to the bodies of other vertebrates, students and scientists often study frogs. Recently, scientists learned that the chemicals some frogs secrete can be used in medicine to fight skin and eye infections.

Frogs are helpful in another way, too. Because they absorb water through their skin, they are often the first creatures to react to pollutants in the water. Frogs that get diseases or can no longer reproduce may give a warning to people about the harmful effects of pollutants in the environment.

Tree frog
catching a fly

Do Frogs Make Good Pets?

Frogs can make good pets. They are colorful, and they are fun to watch as they grow.

But before you get a pet frog, find information at your library or talk to experts at a local pet store. Taking care of frogs can be a lot of work. Some frogs eat only live insects. And frogs can live a long time, so be prepared to care for a pet frog for many years. You should never release a store-bought frog into the wild. It may not be a native to your area, and so it could cause harm to the habitat.

A pet frog can be kept in a mesh- or screen-covered terrarium *(tuh RAIR ee uhm),* which is a transparent container made of glass or plastic. If your pet frog is a type that prefers a dry environment, small pebbles should be placed at the bottom of the container for drainage. Then potting soil and plants can be added. The completed terrarium should be placed in an area that is well lighted but out of direct sunlight.

In addition to frogs, terrariums can hold other amphibian pets, such as toads and salamanders. Pet terrariums need to be kept clean to prevent illness.

Green frog

What's the Difference Between Frogs and Toads?

Frogs and toads have a lot in common. And some frogs even have the word "toad" in their names. No wonder people often confuse them!

Frogs and toads have some major differences, though. Frogs have wet skin. Except for some frogs that burrow, they have long hind legs for jumping. Some frogs can climb trees.

Toads, on the other hand, have dry, warty skin. They are fatter and rounder than frogs, and they have short hind legs. They may hop, but they stay close to the ground.

Frogs and toads have their own separate myths, too. People pretend that if a princess kisses a frog, it will turn into a prince. And they like to say that holding a toad will give you warts. Both ideas are popular myths—but neither one is true.

Toad (right)
with frogs (left)

35

Do Frogs and Toads Have Families?

Neither frogs nor toads live in families. Most provide no care for their eggs or young. However, some adult frogs and toads do guard their eggs against insects, ducks, fish, and other predators. They also care for their eggs until they're ready to hatch.

Some types of female tree frogs carry their eggs on their backs until the eggs are ready to hatch. When the eggs hatch into tadpoles, the females carry them and release them in a pond or stream. Female Surinam toads carry eggs on their backs sunken in their skin. These eggs always hatch into fully-formed frogs called froglets.

Male midwife toads swim with eggs wrapped around themselves. Male Darwin's frogs swallow their mate's eggs and keep them safe in a vocal pouch. There, they develop into tadpoles and then frogs before the male releases them.

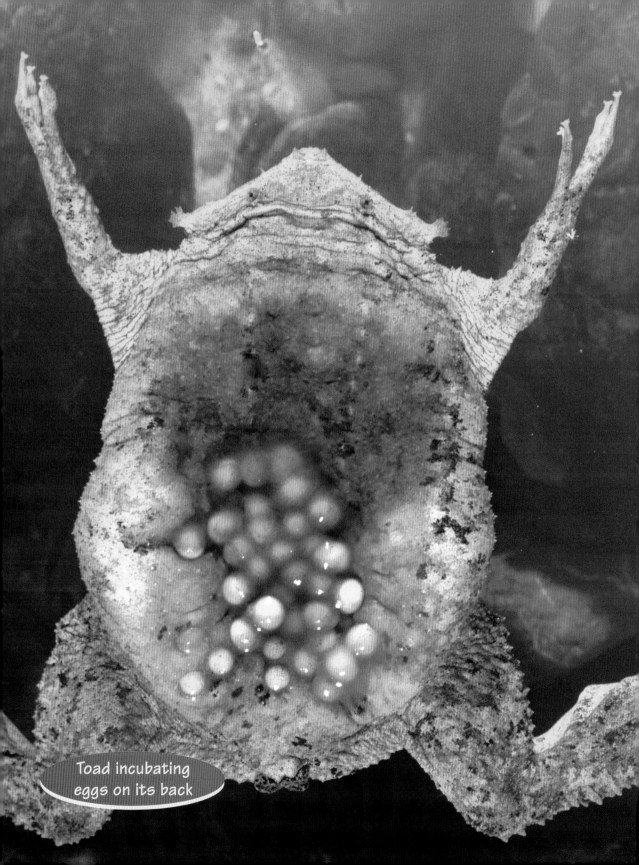

Toad incubating
eggs on its back

Who Keeps That Tadpole Tail?

Like frogs and toads, salamanders are amphibians. Unlike frogs and toads, they keep their tails all their lives.

Salamanders grow up the same way frogs and toads do. They hatch from eggs and emerge as salamander larvae that look a lot like tadpoles. Then they go through metamorphosis. But as adults, they look very different from frogs and toads.

Salamanders look more like lizards than other amphibians. However, they are not dry and scaly as lizards are, and they don't have claws.

Most salamanders lose their gills, grow lungs, and live on land. But some, such as mudpuppies, hellbenders, and congo eels, never become land dwellers. Many of them keep their gills. Some of them never develop lungs.

Marbled salamander

Are Salamanders Fierce?

Salamanders are extremely timid creatures. They do tend to startle people, however. It can be scary to move a pile of leaves or a log and suddenly find a salamander living there.

The habit of hiding in such dark places helped salamanders earn their name. In the Middle Ages, people in Europe sometimes would see salamanders scurry out from piles of logs that were set on fire for heating or cooking. They thought the animals were living in the fire itself. So they called them salamanders, from a Greek word for a mythical lizard that lived in fire.

In fact, salamanders much prefer water. They need to keep their skin moist, and they try to keep their eggs moist, too. They like damp, dark places because the insects they like to eat live there. Salamanders have spots on their skin to help them hide from predators.

Northern red
salamander

What Happened to That Salamander's Tail?

Some kinds of salamanders have an amazing adaptation called autotomy *(aw TOT uh mee)*. If something or someone snags the tail of one of these salamanders, the salamander can make the tail fall off. The salamander can then scoot to safety without its snagged tail!

That is not all that a salamander can do. After a salamander loses its tail, it can regenerate *(ree JEN uhr ayt),* or regrow, a new one. Some salamanders can regenerate legs, too. Some can even regenerate parts of their spinal cord, organs, and eyes.

At first, the new tail or leg or other body part looks pale in comparison to the rest of the salamander. Eventually, the color matches perfectly!

Salamander with
tail regenerating

43

Are Those Salamanders Dancing?

Salamanders are quiet creatures. They don't have a mating call. So when a male salamander finds a female he wants to mate with, he does a dance.

The male salamander waves his tail back and forth in front of the female, and he sends chemical signals her way. If she likes him, she joins the dance.

The two salamanders walk or swim around each other. Sometimes they bump heads, too. Some kinds of male salamanders also hug the females.

Eventually, the male deposits a bundle of sperm nearby and shows the female where it is. She takes the sperm, puts it in her body, and it fertilizes her eggs.

Spotted salamander
courtship dance

45

Are Salamanders Good Parents?

It depends on the type of salamander! Salamanders that live mostly on land just lay their eggs and leave them to their fate. But dusky salamanders and other aquatic salamanders guard their eggs until they hatch.

Usually, the mother aquatic salamander protects the eggs. Among the Japanese giant salamanders, however, the father stays with the eggs.

Not only does the father salamander protect his eggs from predators; he tries to help them grow! He fans them with his tail to create bubbles in the water so the eggs have an oxygen-rich nursery in which to develop.

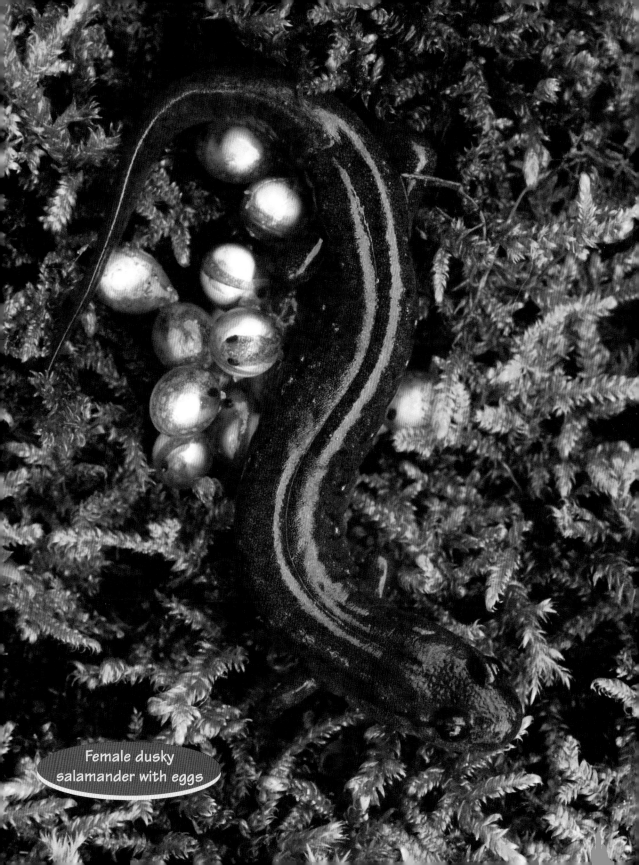

Female dusky
salamander with eggs

Who Is Always on the Lookout?

Like frogs and toads, salamanders must keep an active lookout for predators. They are good at seeing movement. Some can sense movement through their skin. These animals have a good sense of smell, too.

Most salamanders protect themselves by hiding from predators. Some brightly colored salamanders use their coloration to announce that their skin is poisonous. The California slender salamander takes a different approach. It may coil up and spring away.

California slender
salamander coiled

What Is an Eft?

Most salamanders give up aquatic living when they become adults. They return to the water only to lay eggs, but they live on land the rest of the time.

Members of a group of salamanders known as newts are different. After metamorphosis, like other salamanders, newts move to land and begin to mature. After they become adults and return to the water to mate, however, they then may live in the pond or stream for the rest of their lives.

Before it returns to the water to mate, a newt lives and wanders in the forest for years. A young newt in this stage is called an eft. It may take the eft, or migrating *(MY grayt ing)* salamander, anywhere between one and three years to mature to adulthood.

Red eft

Where Do Newts Lay Eggs?

It's usually pretty easy to spot a clutch of salamander eggs. They look like a mound of bubbles or jelly, and you can count each egg.

Red-spotted, or eastern, newts make such counting a little tougher, however. Instead of laying all their eggs at once, these newts go from plant to plant laying one egg at a time. They stick each egg onto a plant with a bit of jellylike substance they produce. It can take months for a spotted newt to lay all of her eggs.

After newt larvae hatch, they remain loners. They stay away from other newts as well as from predators. When they grow into adults, each newt will have its own markings. No two newts will look exactly the same.

Newt developing inside an egg

Why Do Newts Wiggle That Way?

Newts and other salamanders have very short, little legs. Some salamanders that spend a lot of time in the water don't even have back legs. But they do have very flexible bodies. So they make the most of what they have.

On land, newts and salamanders bend their bodies from side to side when they walk. The way they move helps them support their bodies. Their tails are used for support, too. In the water, these animals move their bodies and tails in an S-shape and swim like fish.

Each of these strategies works. Both newts and salamanders can move away quickly when they need to escape.

Crested newt swimming with a wiggling motion

Who Travels Far from Home?

Terrestrial salamanders, the salamanders that live on land, travel far from home after they grow to adulthood. Some have been known to travel several miles from the pond or stream where they hatched.

During breeding season, these salamanders make the long trip back to water to lay their own eggs. Braving predators, harsh weather, and varied terrain, they make their way home. Using their keen sense of smell, they find the exact spot where they were hatched and continue the family tradition.

Some salamanders make the trip every breeding season. Others make the difficult trip home only every other year. And when some kinds of adult newts return to the water, they stay there for good.

Salamander with eggs

Is That a Worm or an Amphibian?

Worms do not have backbones or legs, and they do not go through metamorphosis. For these and other reasons, they are not amphibians. But there is a type of an amphibian that looks like a worm. It's called a caecilian. Caecilians don't have legs as other amphibians do. However, it's really their segmented skin that makes them look like worms.

These creatures, which primarily burrow underground and are hard to find, are different from other amphibians in more ways, too. Their eyes are beneath their skin, and many caecilians have tiny scales embedded in their skin. But they do go through a small metamorphosis. Young caecilians have gills, and adults do not.

Caecilians live only in the tropics. Some can be as long as 5 feet (1.5 meters). Others can be as small as 4 ½ inches (11.4 centimeters).

Caecilian

59

Are Amphibians in Danger?

Frog populations have been declining since the 1980's. Salamander populations are down, too. No one knows exactly why the numbers of these animals are declining, but it's probably the result of many factors.

Because the ozone layer of the atmosphere has thinned, more ultraviolet radiation makes its way to Earth than once did. Frogs' eggs don't hatch when exposed to too much radiation.

Pesticides used in farming kill the animals that amphibians eat and may be harmful to amphibians, too. Many of these chemical pollutants drain into water where amphibians can soak them up.

Amphibians live in marshy areas and wetlands. Many of these have been drained for farmland, housing developments, or corporate office parks. Restored wetlands can do a lot to help amphibians survive.

Red-eyed tree frog

Amphibian Fun Facts

→ Frogs close their eyes when they swallow because they use their eye muscles to help push food down their throats.

→ Some frogs can survive cold so intense that it freezes more than half the water in their bodies.

→ Frogs range in size from a half inch (1.3 centimeters) to almost a foot (30 centimeters) long.

→ The tongues of some salamanders are as long as their bodies.

→ Caecilians' eyes are covered over with skin—and sometimes bone.

→ Salamanders don't have ear holes. Their ears are entirely inside their heads.

→ Amphibians have been around for at least 350 million years.

Glossary

amphibian An animal that spends part of its life on land and the other part in water.

autotomy The ability of an animal to cast off a body part; a salamander can shed its tail.

caecilian An amphibian with a long, wormlike body.

camouflage Features of an animal, such as skin color, that help it blend into its surroundings.

ectotherm An animal whose body temperature is like the temperature of its surroundings.

eft The stage in the life of a newt during which it lives on land.

estivate To sleep when the weather gets too hot and dry.

fertilization The joining together of male and female sex cells to produce a new organism.

frog An amphibian with moist skin and long hind legs.

habitat The area where an animal lives, such as a grassland or wetland.

hibernate To sleep through the cold months.

larva A young form of an animal that looks very different from the adult form.

metamorphosis The process in which a larva changes into an adult animal.

newt A type of salamander with a flatter tail than other salamanders.

regenerate To regrow a body part, such as a tail.

salamander An amphibian with a long, lizardlike body.

tadpole The aquatic, legless larva of a frog or toad.

terrarium A container made of glass or plastic in which pet amphibians are often kept.

toad An amphibian with dry, warty skin and short hind legs.

wetland An area that has water for all or much of the year, such as a marsh or swamp.

63

Index

(**Boldface** indicates a photo, map, or illustration.)

For more information about Frogs and Other Amphibians, try these resources:

Amphibian, an Eyewitness Book, Dorling Kindersley, 2000.

Frogs, by Gail Gibbons, Holiday House, 1994.

From Tadpole to Frog, by Wendy Pfeffer, HarperCollins Juvenile Books, 1994.

http://george.lbl.gov/ITG.hm.pg.docs/Whole.Frog/Whole.Frog.html#intro

http://animaldiversity.ummz.umich.edu/site/topics/frogCalls.html

Amphibian Classification

Scientists classify animals by placing them into groups. The animal kingdom is a group that contains all the world's animals. Phylum, class, order, and family are smaller groups. Each phylum contains many classes. A class contains orders, an order contains families, and a family contains individual species. Each species also has its own scientific name. Here is how the animals in this book fit into this system.

Animals with backbones and their relatives (Phylum Chordata)
Amphibians (Class Amphibia)
Caecilians (Order Gymnophiona)
Frogs and Toads (Order Anura)

Flying frogs (Family Rhacophoridae)

Leptodactylid frogs (Family Leptodactylidae)
Budgett's frog . . . . *Lepidobatrachus laevis*
Argentine horned frog . . . . *Ceratophrys ornata*

Midwife toads (Family Discoglossidae)

Mouth-brooding frogs (Family Rhinodermatidae)
Darwin's frog . . . . *Rhinoderma darwinii*

Pipid frogs (Family Pipidae)
Surinam toad . . . . *Pipa pipa*

Poison-dart frogs (Family Dendrobatidae)
Strawberry poison dart frog . . . . *Dendrobates pumilio*

Toads (Family Bufonidae)

Tree frogs (Family Hylidae)
Gray tree frog . . . . *Hyla versicolor*
Red-eyed tree frog . . . . *Agalychnis callidryas*

True frogs (Family Ranidae)
Green frog . . . . *Rana clamitans*
African bullfrog . . . . *Pyxicephalus adspersus*

Salamanders (Order Caudata)

Congo eels, or amphiumas (Family Amphiumidae)

Hellbenders (Family Cryptobranchidae)
Hellbender . . . . *Cryptobranchus alleganiensis*
Japanese giant salamander . . . . *Andrias japonicus*

Lungless salamanders (Family Plethodontidae)
California slender salamander . . . . *Batrachoseps attenuatus*
Northern red salamander . . . . *Pseudotriton ruber*
Dusky salamander . . . . *Desmognathus fuscus*

Mudpuppies (Family Proteidae)
Mudpuppy . . . . *Necturus maculosus*

Salamanders (Family Salamandridae)
Eastern newt, Spotted newt, Red-spotted newt . . . . *Notophthalmus viridescens*
Crested newt . . . . *Triturus cristatus*

Mole salamanders (Family Ambystomatidae)
Marbled salamander . . . . *Ambystoma opacum*
Spotted salamander . . . . *Ambystoma maculatum*